historical

D0851723

historical tweets

The Completely Unabridged and Ridiculously Brief History of the World

Alan Beard and Alec McNayr

Villard Trade Paperbacks Ⓥ New York

A Villard Books Trade Paperback Original

Copyright © 2010 by Alan Beard and Alec McNayr

All rights reserved.

Published in the United States by Villard Books, an imprint of The Random House Publishing Group, a division of Random House, Inc., New York.

VILLARD and "V" CIRCLED Design are registered trademarks of Random House, Inc.

LIBRARY OF CONGRESS CATALOGING-IN-PUBLICATION DATA

Beard, Alan
Historical tweets: the completely unabridged and ridiculously brief history of the world /
Alan Beard and Alec McNayr.
p.   cm.
ISBN 978-0-345-52263-4
1. History—Humor. 2. Twitter—Humor. I. McNayr, Alec. II. Title.
PN6231.H47B43 2010   818'.602—dc22   2010007630

Printed in the United States of America

www.villard.com

9 8 7 6 5 4 3 2 1

To our wives, Sharon and Katie

5:06 PM April 27, 2010 from HistoricalTweets.com

AlanandAlec
Alan Beard and Alec McNayr

Henry VIII
They sound wonderful, but I'd probably still kill them.

Ray Charles
Are they as hot as I imagine them to be?

Ike Turner
I'd hit that.

contents

introduction

History books have been ruining history. So much analysis. So much effort to put events into proper context. So many unnecessary words.

Then, just when scholars had given up hope that history could again fascinate the electronically addled and pop culture–obsessed current citizens of planet Earth, we uncovered a side of history that had long been rumored but never confirmed: the tweets of bygone eras.

The world might never have known what is now accepted as irrefutable fact: Tweets have existed since the dawn of time. From the ancients to the space robots and every leader and thinker in between, tweets have been the dominant communication platform for the sharing of an embarrassing confession, a hidden truth, an iconic observation, or an untimely boast.

Now, with *Historical Tweets,* history's most amazing men and women can be fully understood, 140 characters at a time. You're welcome.

Cro-Magnum, P.I.

pet rocks

drag by hair

hottest clubs

Me cold now.

cavewoman naked

cave refinancing

apple recipes

Big Bang loud

hunting

opposable thumbs

Why fire go out?

saber-tooth necklaces

grunt translator

wi-fire hot spots

gathering

What is wheel?

woolly mammoth weak spot

bronto ribs

original Jurassic parks

@God OMY! I'm naked!

3:11 PM July 22, 843234040 BC from tweeden

Adam1
Adam

Replies to **Adam1**

Eve @adam1 For the last time, my eyes are up here.

6:04 PM January 25, 843234039 BC from tweeden

Horse @adam1 What's a stallion got to do to keep you from riding bareback?

12:36 PM February 17, 843234039 BC from tweeden

3-Toed Sloth @adam1 You followed the awesome names giraffe and zebra by naming me 3-toed sloth? Weak, man. So very weak.

10:35 AM March 3, 843234039 BC from tweeden

Snake @adam1 You'll never get viruses if you go with Apple.

11:41 PM July 21, 843234039 BC from tweeden

Breaking up is hard to do.

11:21 PM October 8, 500694621 BC from crackberry

TheContinental
Pangea

4

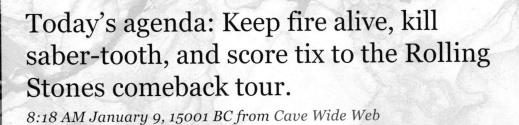

Today's agenda: Keep fire alive, kill saber-tooth, and score tix to the Rolling Stones comeback tour.

8:18 AM January 9, 15001 BC from Cave Wide Web

cave_man
Brog

5

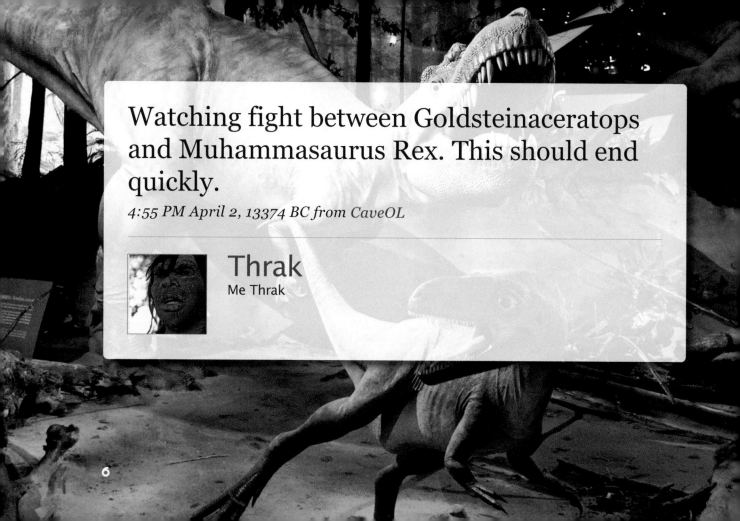

Watching fight between Goldsteinaceratops and Muhammasaurus Rex. This should end quickly.

4:55 PM April 2, 13374 BC from CaveOL

Thrak
Me Thrak

Cro-Magnon kids giggle nonstop every time I say "Homo erectus."

2:15 PM September 17, 13358 BC from TweetSkool

1st_Teacher

Mrs. Mwarak

7

Other caveboys want to hunt and chase fire. My passions are interior design and show tunes. #cavepride

4:27 PM August 5, 9816 BC from Tweetie

Grok
Grok Grak

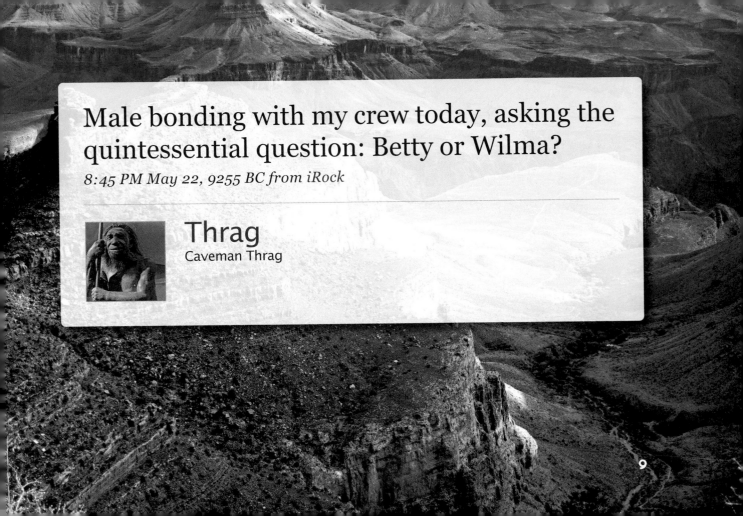

Male bonding with my crew today, asking the quintessential question: Betty or Wilma?

8:45 PM May 22, 9255 BC from iRock

Thrag
Caveman Thrag

T-Rex At the heart of my rage is the inability to do push-ups. #armstooshort
3:22 PM January 30, 30890546 BC from Twittersaurus

 T-Rex Career thumb-war record: 0–248. #armstooshort
3:40 PM January 30, 30890546 BC from Twittersaurus

 T-Rex Canceled subscription to Playboy. #armstooshort
4:10 PM January 30, 30890546 BC from Twittersaurus

 T-Rex Unable to properly flip the pterodactyl. #armstooshort
4:52 PM January 30, 30890546 BC from Twittersaurus

Ark was already full, so I had to tell the dragons, dinosaurs, and unicorns I'd be "right back to pick them up." #mybad #extinction

10:55 AM April 28, 6345 BC from tweetflood

CapnFlood
Noah

sandal sale

toga party

monotheism

pyramid design

hemlock antidote

sword-control legislation

Helen of Troy naked

samurai movies

Judas sucks

What does BC mean?

Doric or Ionic

vomitorium etiquette

Colosseum tickets

Constantinople rebrand

new chariot smell

camel racing

NAMBLA

Pompeii vacation package

Spartan ab blaster

Rolling Stones tickets

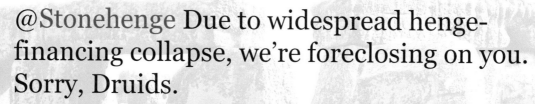

@Stonehenge Due to widespread henge-financing collapse, we're foreclosing on you. Sorry, Druids.

11:31 AM November 2, 2986 BC from bankruptwee

Celticwide
Celticwide, Inc.

14

Every time I wear my baggy pants and gold chains, everyone calls out "Go Hammur, go, Hammur, Code!"

8:44 PM February 27, 1780 BC from Canttouchthis

HammurTime
Hammurabi

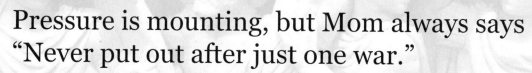

Pressure is mounting, but Mom always says "Never put out after just one war."

10:56 PM May 20, 1235 BC from troytter

HoT
Helen of Troy

16

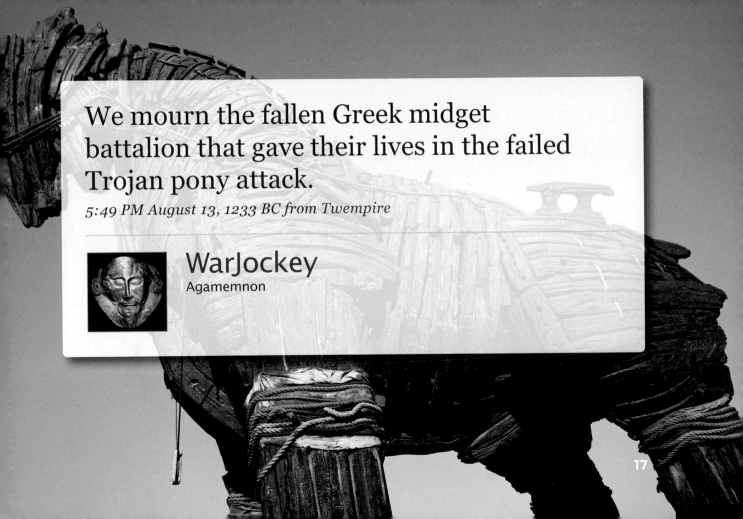

We mourn the fallen Greek midget battalion that gave their lives in the failed Trojan pony attack.

5:49 PM August 13, 1233 BC from Twempire

WarJockey
Agamemnon

17

Once I destroy this tiny shepherd, all will know that size and power always prevail. The "Goliath and David" metaphor will last forever.

8:55 PM September 15, 1022 BC from Giant URL

Go!-Liath
Goliath

Having a hard time explaining to my wife why the maid's breasts are suddenly solid gold.

10:21 PM April 22, 714 BC from 14CaratTweet

TheTouch
King Midas

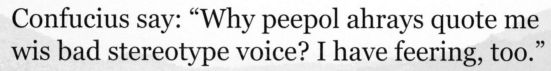

Confucius say: "Why peepol ahrays quote me wis bad stereotype voice? I have feering, too."

8:44 AM March 23, 488 BC from philosotwee

SoQuotable
Confucius

shrug

3:35 PM October 20, 452 BC from Randtweets

EarthSquats
Atlas

The newly opened Acropolis is an eyesore. One can only hope its ultramodern architecture will soon be forgotten.

12:58 PM May 15, 445 BC from acropotweets

ColumnAsISee_em
Eustathios

22

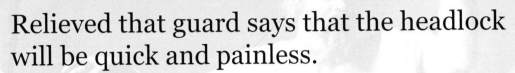

Relieved that guard says that the headlock will be quick and painless.

7:23 PM October 1, 399 BC from sotweetic method

Socrazy
Socrates

23

So tired of the "let's just be friends" talk.

9:33 PM February 14, 398 BC from *fun factory*

Mentalist
Plato

24

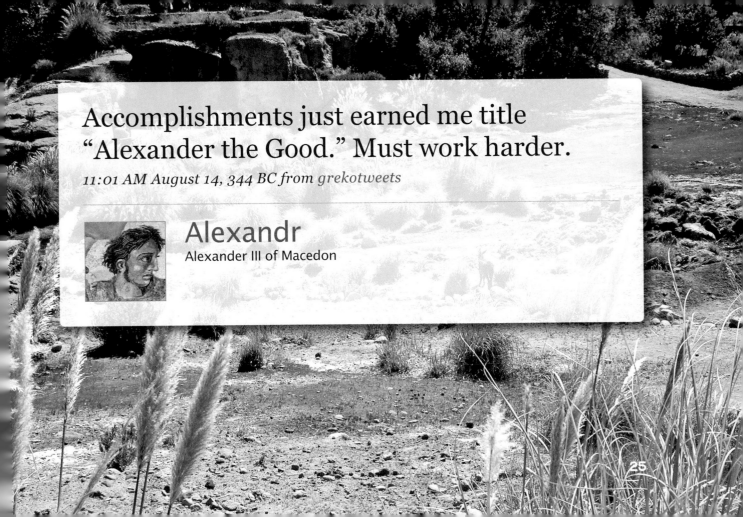

Accomplishments just earned me title "Alexander the Good." Must work harder.

11:01 AM August 14, 344 BC from grekotweets

Alexandr
Alexander III of Macedon

25

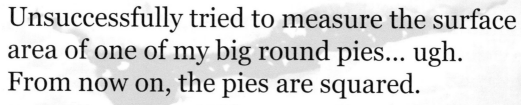

Unsuccessfully tried to measure the surface area of one of my big round pies... ugh. From now on, the pies are squared.

11:03 AM November 22, 256 BC from tweetmatician

MeasureMan
Archimedes

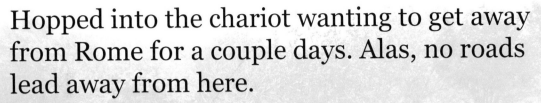

Hopped into the chariot wanting to get away from Rome for a couple days. Alas, no roads lead away from here.

4:27 PM August 9, 56 BC from MySalad

RomanRuler
Julius Caesar

27

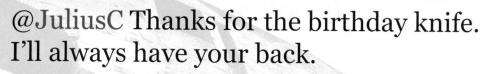

@JuliusC Thanks for the birthday knife.
I'll always have your back.

3:43 PM March 14, 44 BC from Roman Twempire

8–2
Brutus

Accidentally turned wine into water.
This party sucks now. #mybad

9:59 PM March 21, 31 from BiblicalTweets.com

JC33
Jesus of Nazareth

29

3 advances and retweets

bubonic plague cures

Crusades news

round tables

Luther smackdown

Manhattan real estate

Elizabeth I naked

Rolling Stones tickets

Round Earth theory

Robin Hood

vikings before favre

West Indies Hotties

religious freedom

Da Vinci patents

Shakespeare CliffsNotes

team romeo

prank guillotines Brittany spears

London Fire Department FAIL

Plymouth Rock location

95 theses rap lyrics

Spilled beard growth potion all over my lap. Now my "little wizard" is a Hairy Peter.

11:28 PM February 13, 516 from Twitter Magic

TheWiz
Merlin

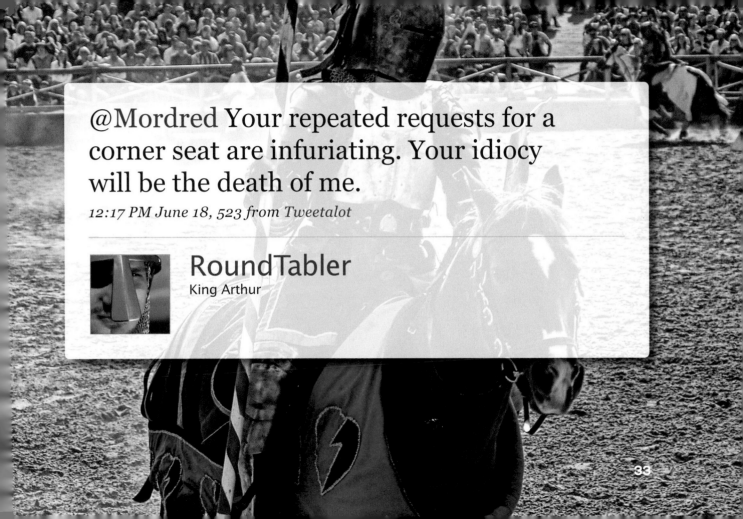

@Mordred Your repeated requests for a corner seat are infuriating. Your idiocy will be the death of me.

12:17 PM June 18, 523 from Tweetalot

RoundTabler
King Arthur

33

To reduce complaints from our female fans and boost our street cred among neighboring villages, we will now be RAPPING and pillaging.

10:10 PM September 20, 980 from V.W.A.

Brutish_Horde
Vikings

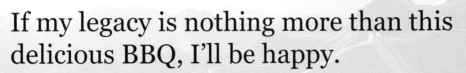

If my legacy is nothing more than this delicious BBQ, I'll be happy.

12:46 PM July 14, 1223 from siberian tweets

ShockaKhan
Genghis Khan

35

Finally arrived in China. Feel like a fish out of water.

5:35 AM February 15, 1297 from Boost Mobile

Marco!
Marco Polo

Forgot the sunscreen at home. OMG, I'll never be burned worse than I am now.

1:15 PM September 1, 1429 from Twittervisions

Joanie
Joan of Arc

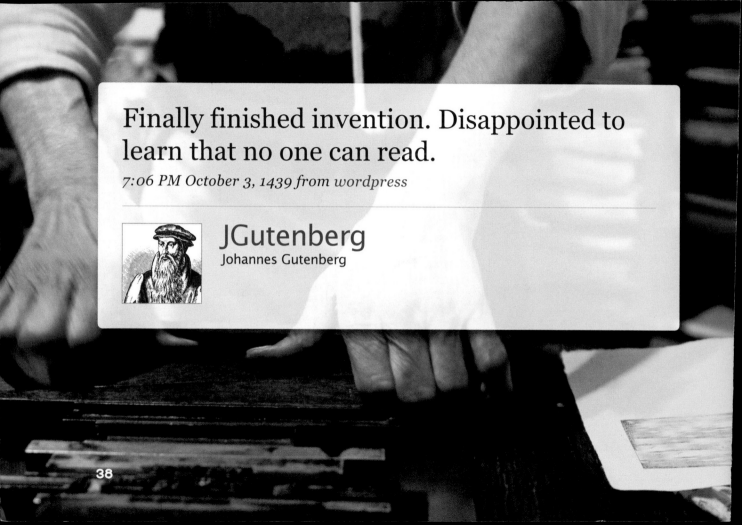

Finally finished invention. Disappointed to learn that no one can read.

7:06 PM October 3, 1439 from wordpress

JGutenberg
Johannes Gutenberg

38

Several men injured today when, after what seemed like a light collision, the rear end of Pinta burst into flames. #unsafeatanyspeed

4:10 PM October 16, 1492 from new world tweets

Columbo
Christopher Columbus

Advice for young artists: Visit the site before quoting a price for a "simple ceiling paint job."

4:45 PM December 24, 1511 from Sistween Chapel

ArtyMike
Michelangelo

40

@Michelangelo I'll never forgive you for sculpting me the moment I got out of the pool...

3:14 PM October 26, 1504 from Tiny URL

ChiseledAbs
The David

These new shoe inserts are incredibly comfortable.

9:30 AM March 5, 1519 *from Dr. Tweets*

LikeaFelon

Magellan

Today I may die, but my vengeance shall flow for centuries.

2:55 PM July 1, 1520 from *Tweetie #2*

Mexiking
Montezuma

What would I do without match.com?

10:34 PM June 2, 1540 from tweeter of london

Henry8
King Henry VIII

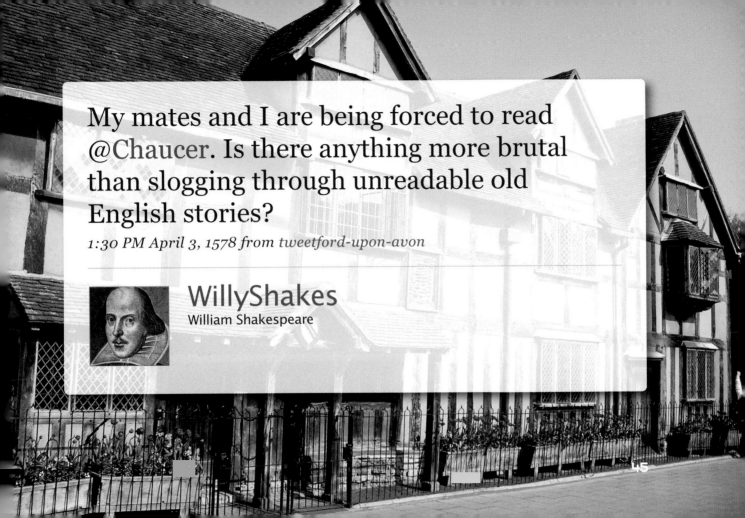

My mates and I are being forced to read @Chaucer. Is there anything more brutal than slogging through unreadable old English stories?

1:30 PM April 3, 1578 from tweetford-upon-avon

WillyShakes
William Shakespeare

Took an hour to get that bird crap out of my hair. Think I'll change it to "apple" when I tell the story.

7:05 PM July 6, 1666 from Apple Newton

Gravitas
Isaac Newton

Thinking of opening a cake store. It will make a killing.

11:22 AM October 12, 1793 from TweetCake

MarieAntoinette
Marie Antoinette

47

4

revolutionary and industrial tweets

cavalry training

tea party costumes

cherry tree repair

newfangled steam engine

Redcoats

oral carpentry

Martha Washington naked

robber barons

flag patterns

Rolling Stones tickets

map to
Carnegie Hall

famous last stands

Original Darwin Awards

President Davis

Wyatt Earp training video

Honoré de Balzac

sweat shops

Oregon Trail video game

Kitty Hawk runway

gold panning

Natives love the bling.

2:08 PM May 27, 1626 from twinkets

ManhattanBuyer
Peter Minuit

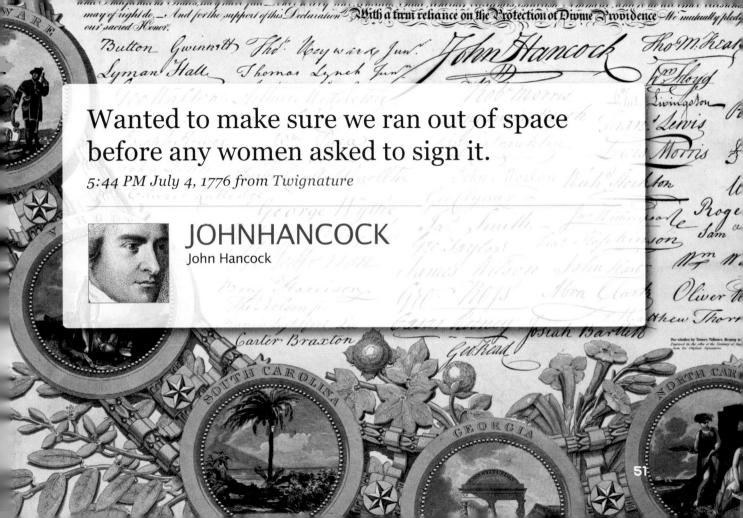

Wanted to make sure we ran out of space before any women asked to sign it.

5:44 PM July 4, 1776 from Twignature

JOHNHANCOCK
John Hancock

51

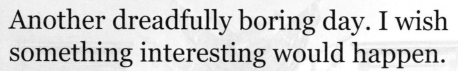

Another dreadfully boring day. I wish something interesting would happen.

9:09 PM July 4, 1776 from kinglytweets

george3
King George III

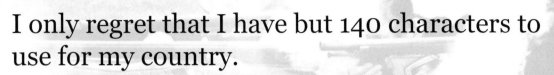

I only regret that I have but 140 characters to use for my country.

4:58 PM September 22, 1776 from Tweath Row

HaleNo
Nathan Hale

53

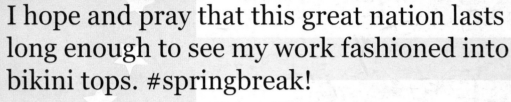

I hope and pray that this great nation lasts long enough to see my work fashioned into bikini tops. #springbreak!

3:26 PM March 24, 1779 from Stars & Tweets Forever

FlagLady
Betsy Ross

It's all about the me's, baby.

8:11 PM December 17, 1781 from tweetkite

BeFrank
Benjamin Franklin

Hoping my "right to sexy slaves" won't get cut from what I've dubbed the Bill of Oh-So-Rights.

11:34 AM September 7, 1787 from tweetstitutional

TJeffUSA
Thomas Jefferson

Hungover again. Nothing good can come from my addiction to gin.

7:07 AM May 1, 1787 from twitterberry

Cottontale
Eli Whitney

57

Dentist delivered the bad news: termites.

10:47 AM August 9, 1791 from Cherry Twee

GWash
George Washington

@aaronburr Nice shot...

7:39 AM July 11, 1804 from tweehawken

AlexHamilton
Alexander Hamilton

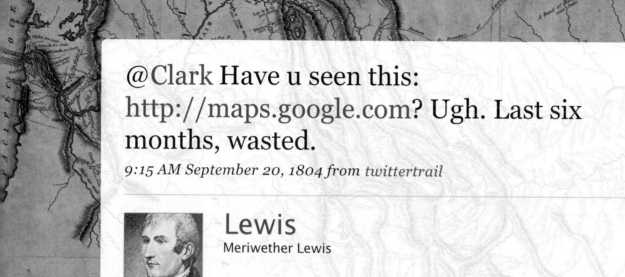

@Clark Have u seen this: http://maps.google.com? Ugh. Last six months, wasted.

9:15 AM September 20, 1804 from twittertrail

Lewis
Meriwether Lewis

Can anyone recommend a cure for persistent nipple itch?

3:11 PM May 15, 1812 from twittere

Napoleon
Napoleon Bonaparte

61

.. /..-. .- -. - . -.. .-.-.- LOL

7:40 PM September 10, 1837 from morsetweets

... --
Samuel Morse

Another bird stuck in my study—it's what I get for leaving the window open. Calling animal control.

8:49 PM January 2, 1845 from poetwee

Poeboy
Edgar Allan Poe

Sorry for the lack of tweets. Wi-fi sucks underground.

7:14 AM August 18, 1850 from Tweedom

Conductor
Harriet Tubman

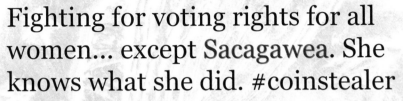

Fighting for voting rights for all women... except Sacagawea. She knows what she did. #coinstealer

6:38 PM April 23, 1868 from TweetCoin

RockTheVote
Susan B. Anthony

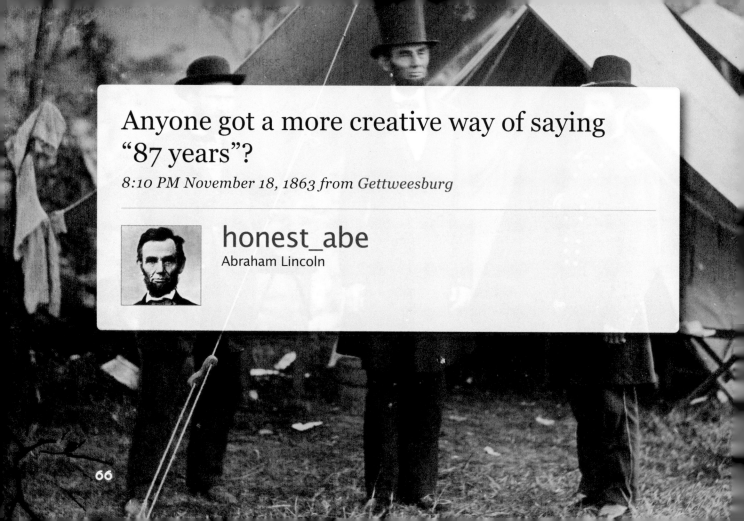

Anyone got a more creative way of saying "87 years"?

8:10 PM November 18, 1863 from Gettweesburg

honest_abe
Abraham Lincoln

66

Replies to @**honest_abe**

Albert Einstein @honest_abe A relative amount of space-time ago...

6:22 AM December 22, 1926 from twee=mc2

George Lucas @honest_abe "A long time ago at a battlefield far, far away."

9:30 AM April 30, 1977 from jarjartweets

Stephen Hawking @honest_abe I've got nothing for 87, but I do know $(87 \times 87 \times 10) + 4395 = 80085$.

5:39 PM October 30, 2003 from tweeticist

Bill Clinton @stephenhawking [high five]

11:06 PM August 4, 1997 from tweetsax

67

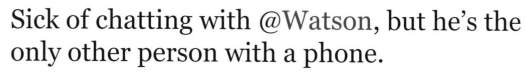

Sick of chatting with @Watson, but he's the only other person with a phone.

11:03 AM March 10, 1876 from tweetephone

alexGB
Alexander Graham Bell

gr8 show tonite. The Ford is the perfect venue for AAAAARRGH!!

10:14 PM April 14, 1865 from Tweet Theatre

honest_abe
Abraham Lincoln

69

@sitting_bull I warn you in advance, this battle will make me famous.

4:01 PM June 23, 1876 from Twittle Big Horn

GenCuster
George Custer

70

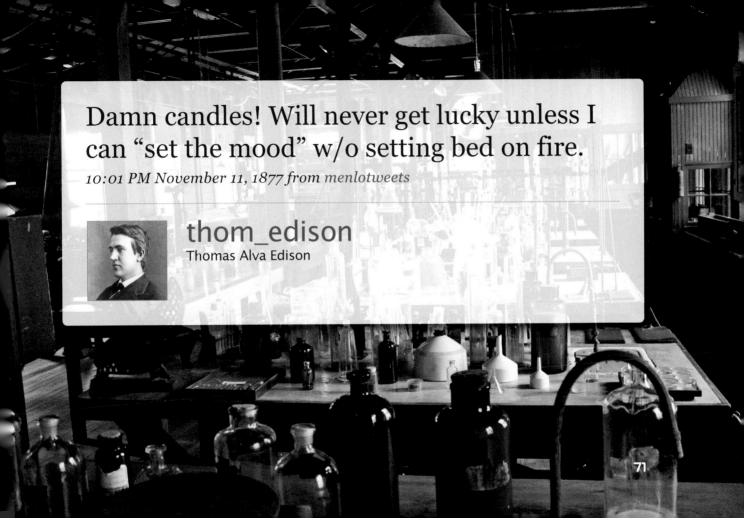

Damn candles! Will never get lucky unless I can "set the mood" w/o setting bed on fire.

10:01 PM November 11, 1877 from menlotweets

thom_edison
Thomas Alva Edison

71

Critic just said my new work was exciting and gay. LOL

9:30 PM September 23, 1881 from earnesttweets

wilde_man
Oscar Wilde

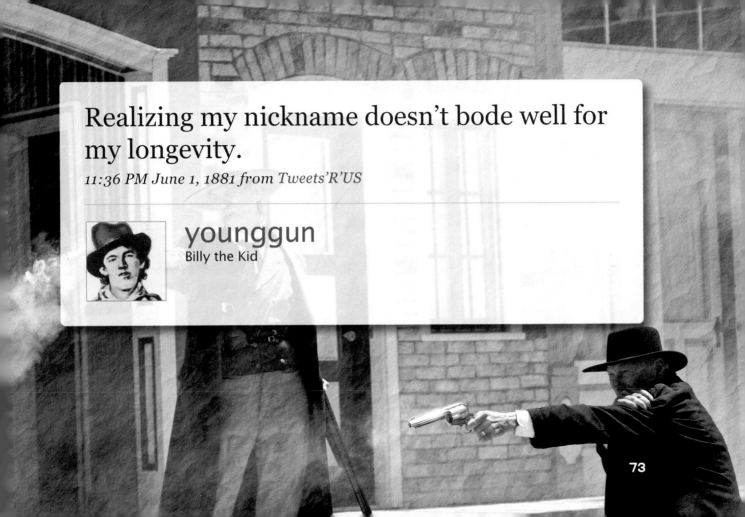

Realizing my nickname doesn't bode well for my longevity.

11:36 PM June 1, 1881 from Tweets'R'US

younggun
Billy the Kid

73

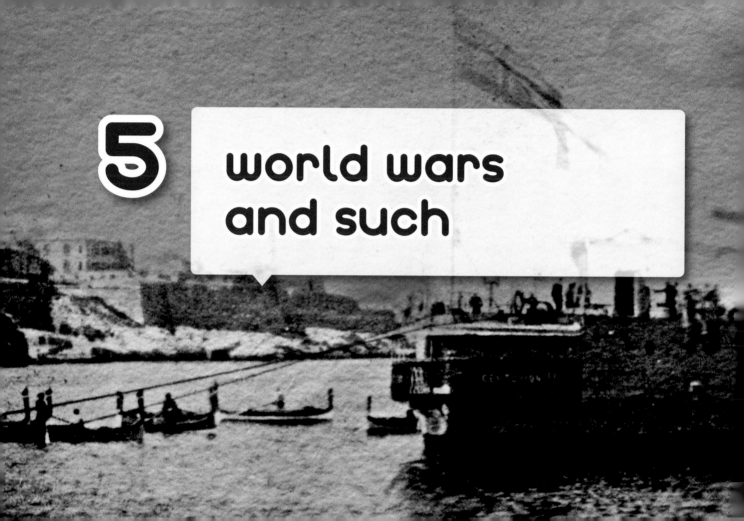

flapper dresses

Tristan Ludlow

other infamous days

hot stock tips

trench warmers

Tokyo Rose radio hour

Hitler naked

new deals

Wrathy Grapes

fastest
bread line

FDR's on a roll.

flask concealment

speakeasy passwords

Pimp My Model T

Keystone Kops YouTube

We Want You

jobs

What does "margin call" mean?

Edsel return policy

hottest books about book burning

Nothing I love more than a good Ethiopian joke. Their extreme malnutrition is completely hilarious.

10:44 AM January 30, 1906 from MiracleWorker

TalktotheHand
Helen Keller

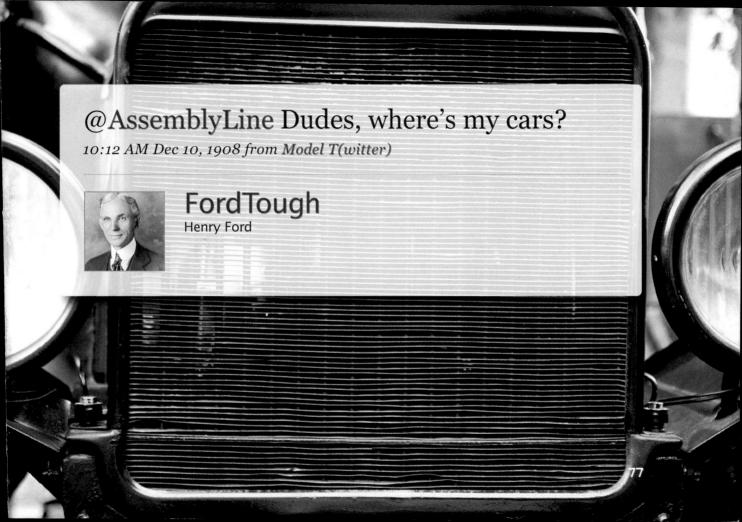

@AssemblyLine Dudes, where's my cars?

10:12 AM Dec 10, 1908 from Model T(witter)

FordTough
Henry Ford

77

Gandhi Punched an old lady today. Felt amazing.
10:36 PM May 22, 1947 from Pacitweets

Mother Teresa @gandhi punched me today.
10:36 PM May 22, 1947 from Tweresa

Princess Diana Punched an old lady today. Felt amazing.
4:42 PM November 19, 1993 from Twittingham Palace

Paul Newman @di punched me today.
4:42 PM November 19, 1993 from Twitman's Own

My drink's STILL warm. What's a girl to do to get some ice around here? #titanicfail

7:44 PM April 13, 1912 from RMS Tweetanic

MOllyBr0wn
Molly Brown

8:40 PM November 29, 1924 from pantotweet

Honky

Harpo Marx

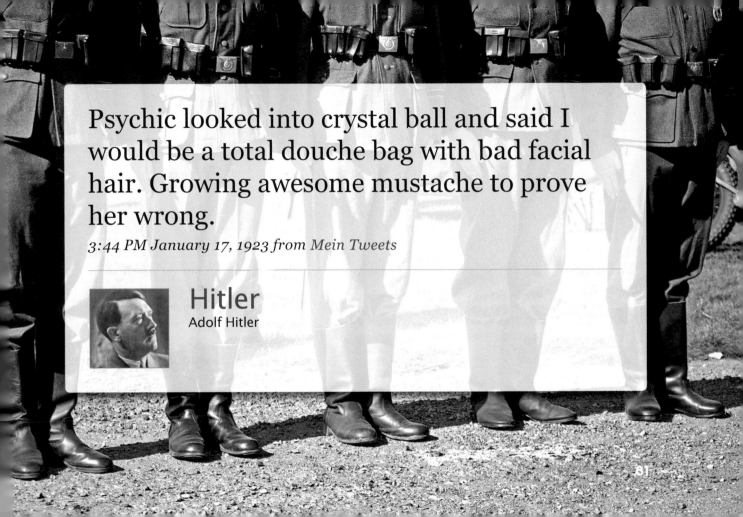

Psychic looked into crystal ball and said I would be a total douche bag with bad facial hair. Growing awesome mustache to prove her wrong.

3:44 PM January 17, 1923 from Mein Tweets

Hitler
Adolf Hitler

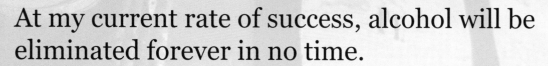

At my current rate of success, alcohol will be eliminated forever in no time.

3:31 PM October 17, 1931 from prohitwition

Nesster
Eliot Ness

© JANU

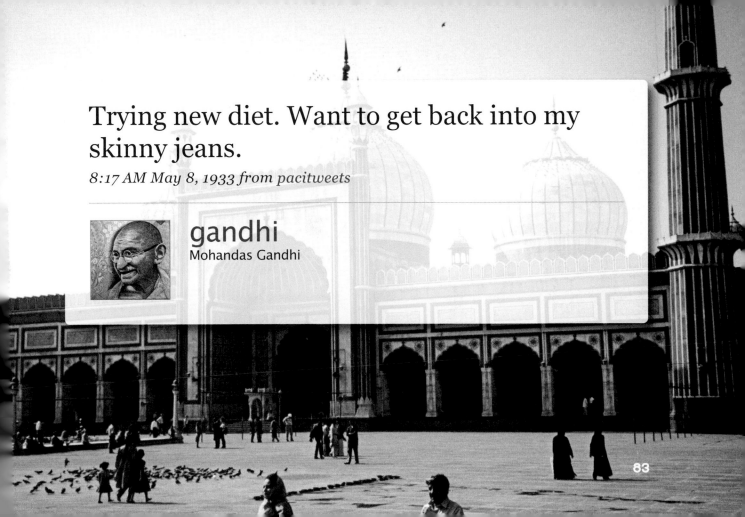

Trying new diet. Want to get back into my skinny jeans.

8:17 AM May 8, 1933 from pacitweets

gandhi
Mohandas Gandhi

83

@FDR WEH CAN HAZ JOBZ NOW?

10:33 AM March 4, 1933 from the great twepression

Unemployed
American Workforce

84

@Bonnie We're the rarest of breeds: heroic outlaws. No way this ends badly.

4:01 PM May 19, 1934 from Twittaway Car

Clyde
Clyde Barrow

85

Coach just assured me gold medal winner
gets to kick @Hitler in the balls. #motivation

6:30 AM June 4, 1936 from USA Tweet & Field

BerlinBolt
Jesse Owens

Flying high after the world's largest airship was named in my honor, its majesty symbolic of Germany's unforgettable accomplishments.

9:37 PM May 3, 1937 from Tweet Deck

Hindenburg
Paul von Hindenburg

87

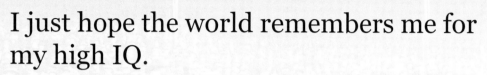

I just hope the world remembers me for my high IQ.

10:01 PM October 1, 1940 from sultanoftweet

The_Babe
Babe Ruth

Realtime search results for **D-Day**

Dwight D. Eisenhower @Troops Yes, D-Day. D-Did I stutter?
10:15 PM June 6, 1944 from Twentagon

Rock Hudson Had to make out with D-Day today.
5:41 PM May 21, 1959 from Pillow Twalk

John F. Kennedy Secret Service codc for meet-ups with Marilyn: Double-D Day.
11:17 PM October 9, 1962 from Twennedy

Hugh Hefner Every day is Double-D Day for me.
3:51 PM February 13, 1985 from The Mansion

@Diary Forgot to put my iPhone on vibrate. Tense few minutes there.

5:33 PM January 8, 1944 from Verstecken von dem Bösen

Anne_Frank
Anne Frank

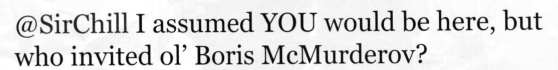

@SirChill I assumed YOU would be here, but who invited ol' Boris McMurderov?

8:03 AM February 4, 1945 from Yaltahoo!

FDR
President Franklin D. Roosevelt

My detractors must not realize how difficult it is to do ANYTHING 25 million times.

1:17 PM August 16, 1950 from St. Twetersburg

HammerNSickle

Joseph Stalin

Dewey defeats Truman, then mockingly jabs, "Loser gets the library decimal system!"

6:48 AM November 3, 1948 from newstweet

chicagodailytribune
Chicago Daily Tribune

6 turbulent tweets

Woodstock regrets

LSD side effects

giant leaps

Where is Vietnam?

Adam West poop crazy

Don Draper naked

Russian dog satellite

how to tie-dye

three-hour tour

Buzz Aldrin
beat-down video

Movin' on Up mp3

bra-burning techniques

bus boycott schedule

Marilyn NYC sidewalk pics

Black Panther sign-ups

Saturday night
comedy live

morning napalm

"whites only" sign removal service

#munichfail

secret hiking maps to Canada

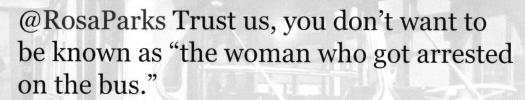

@RosaParks Trust us, you don't want to be known as "the woman who got arrested on the bus."

7:12 AM December 1, 1955 from BusTweet

MTA2857
Montgomery Bus #2857

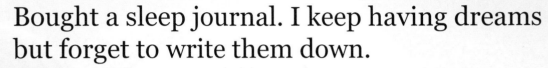

Bought a sleep journal. I keep having dreams but forget to write them down.

11:19 PM June 4, 1960 from Mountaintwop

martinlkjr
Martin Luther King, Jr.

Just locked up Levi's sponsorship. So remember, Black Panthers: Buy any jeans necessary.

11:55 AM October 4, 1959 from Nation of Twislam

X
Malcolm X

First draft: Float like a butterfly, sting like a well-constructed insult. Thoughts?

2:30 PM October 29, 1960 from TweetKO

Ali
Muhammad Ali

99

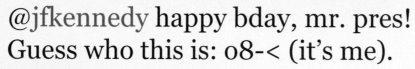

@jfkennedy happy bday, mr. pres!
Guess who this is: o8-< (it's me).

9:39 PM May 29, 1962 from twitterflirt

Marilyn!
Marilyn Monroe

New girlfriend. Bandmates are going to love her.

4:44 PM November 15, 1966 from tweatles

Imaginer
John Lennon

Launching new start-up. Looking for silent pardners.

11:45 AM June 1, 1967 from Wild Twest

TheDuke
John Wayne

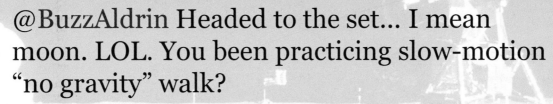

@BuzzAldrin Headed to the set... I mean moon. LOL. You been practicing slow-motion "no gravity" walk?

6:44 AM July 17, 1969 from one tweet for man

AstroNeil
Neil Armstrong

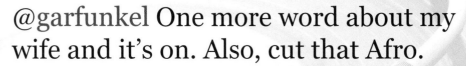

@garfunkel One more word about my
wife and it's on. Also, cut that Afro.

9:59 AM August 29, 1969 from 2ndBase

MrRobinson
Jackie Robinson

What to wear, what to wear...

11:53 PM January 13, 1971 from itweeteverywhere

johnny$
Johnny Cash

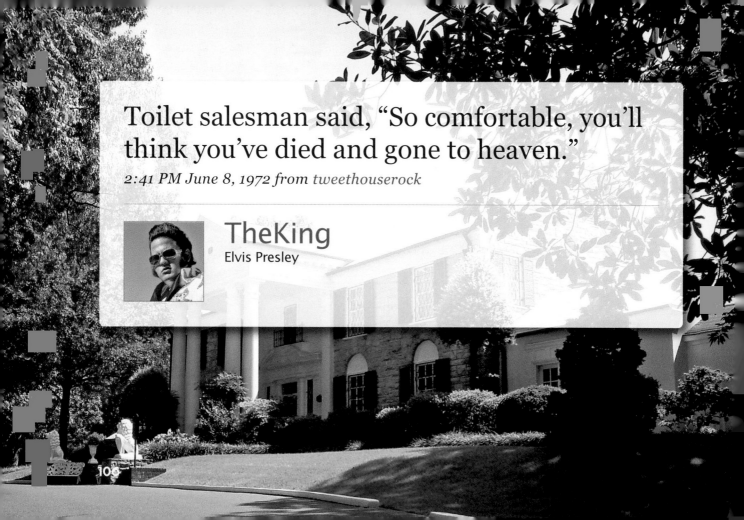

Toilet salesman said, "So comfortable, you'll think you've died and gone to heaven."

2:41 PM June 8, 1972 from tweethouserock

TheKing
Elvis Presley

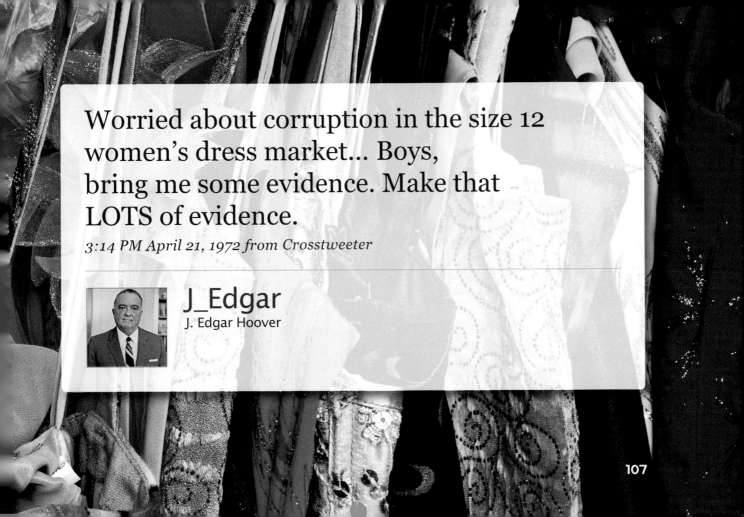

Worried about corruption in the size 12
women's dress market... Boys,
bring me some evidence. Make that
LOTS of evidence.

3:14 PM April 21, 1972 from Crosstweeter

J_Edgar
J. Edgar Hoover

Dumped by first girlfriend. Don't worry,
I rebound easily.

5:55 PM April 20, 1955 from 20k Tweets

TheStilt
Wilt Chamberlain

Realtime search results for **#thegreatest**

 Ali Just smoked @JoeFrasier. I'll say it again. I am #thegreatest of all time.
1:17 PM October 1, 1975 from twitta in manila

 Great Fire of London @Ali So you smoked one guy... I torched an entire city. #thegreatest
2:37 AM September 6, 1666 from Twitterblaze

 Great Wall of China @Ali Can YOU be seen from space? #thegreatest
11:42 AM March 19, 210 BC from Tweetgolia

 Great Depression @Ali Dudes literally jumping out of windows. All I have to say. #thegreatest
6:48 PM January 21, 1941 from Twelfare Line

7 modern tweets

skinny ties

Mondale FTW

roids

LL vs. Kool Moe Dee

grunge flannel

Rick Astley music video

Madonna not naked

anything
Oprah does

junk bond broker

Miami Vice shirts

Beta owners club

first half-white
president

leg warmer sale

convert LP to cassette

one-armed drummer

Flipper Nation

flux capacitor

B. A. Baracus sleeping pills

dotcom stock portfolio

New Coke recipe

@RadioStar You're dead!

12:01 AM August 1, 1983 from MTweeV

Video
Music Videos

About to go on stage. @BubblesTheChimp
ate one of my gloves. What now?

7:33 PM April 14, 1983 from twiller

OneGlove
Michael Jackson

@Reagan You love Robitussin, I love Sudafed. Let's just agree to disagree and end this cold war.

7:19 AM February 10, 1985 from commutweets

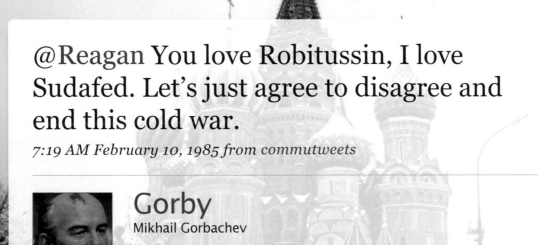

Gorby
Mikhail Gorbachev

Team dietitian says the key to becoming a champion is more Rice.

9:12 AM April 30, 1985 from forty-tweeters

JoeMont49
Joe Montana

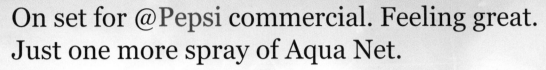

On set for @Pepsi commercial. Feeling great.
Just one more spray of Aqua Net.

9:11 AM February 10, 1984 from twiller

BillyJeansLvr
Michael Jackson

Had to use my A.K. Bad day.

11:38 PM May 23, 1992 from tweetlife

IceCube
Ice Cube

About to meet with witness protection.
Wish me luck.

8:45 AM September 2, 1996 from all tweetz on me

Tupac
Tupac Shakur

I invented Twitter.

6:12 PM March 9, 1999 from Inconvenient Tweets

Algorithm
Al Gore

@Saddam Just hang in there.

8:43 AM December 30, 2006 from cavetweets

BinHidin

Osama bin Laden

@barrybonds Congrats on 756—you earned it! [wink]

9:04 PM August 7, 2007 from tweetrage

jose4040
José Canseco

Retired superstars like me mostly hang out in bars.

11:05 AM December 5, 2008 from OJail

the_juiceman
O. J. Simpson

122

@Obama WEH STIL HAZ NO JOBZ

1:32 PM April 27, 2010 from Still Depressed

Unemployed
American Workforce

123

8

epilogue: making history

Submit Your Own Tweet

We've received hundreds of historical tweets from our readers. Submit your own at our oh-so-easy-to-use website: HistoricalTweets.com.

Here's one to get you started: What did Elvis tweet after meeting President Nixon in the White House?

3:32 PM December 21, 1970 from wi-house

TheKing
Elvis Presley

Hate Tweets

Uncovering history's secrets takes a clear head and a firm resolve, so we're unflinchingly fearless in our relentless pursuit of the truth. Here is a sampling of the hate tweets we've received... keep 'em coming.

Joseph Stalin I was just chatting with @Satan and we agree that your book sucks.

12:01 AM January 20, 2009 from Hatees

Dan Brown Putting words into the mouths of historical figures is unconscionable. You should be ashamed of yourselves.

8:14 AM September 15, 2009 from DanVinci Code

Ken Burns I hate everything about your book and site, but mostly I hate your brevity and lack of bangs. #140hoursorless

2:58 PM July 4, 2009 from the Me Effect

Smithsonian We are delighted to inform you that your book is being placed in each of our Smithsonian locations... just in case we run out of toilet paper.

4:59 PM April 27, 2010 from NaturalHistwee

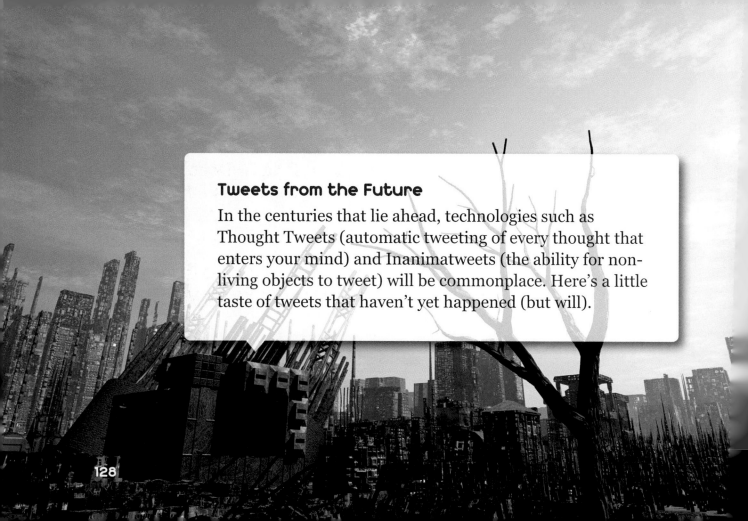

Tweets from the Future

In the centuries that lie ahead, technologies such as Thought Tweets (automatic tweeting of every thought that enters your mind) and Inanimatweets (the ability for non-living objects to tweet) will be commonplace. Here's a little taste of tweets that haven't yet happened (but will).

Twitter Visit us at our new home: twitter.google.com
3:11 PM May 25, 2011 from exit strategy

Chicago Times In the 500th annual Biggest Douche Bag Ever contest, @Hitler remains undefeated. Will anyone ever knock him off his throne?
7:03 AM December 1, 2445 from digitalnews

Robot Overlord 01001001 00100000 01100110 01100001 01110010 01110100 01100101 01100100 00101110
6:44 PM April 17, 2850 from binary tweets

Astronaut Jones Watching the Goldsteinobot-XJ9 fight the Islaminator-5000. Hope this ends soon.
8:45 PM September 23, 3319 from orbitaltweets

acknowledgments

First off, we'd like to thank the HistoricalTweets.com fans who forwarded, replied, commented, and retweeted our work around the Web. Thank you to all the photographers who graciously gave us permission to use their work, and thanks to the ones who were snooty about it but then caved in. Big ups to Darnell Brisco for his heavy lifting; our agent, Kate McKean; our editor, Ryan Doherty, and the rest of the hard-working team at Random House (especially Liz Cosgrove); and, of course, thanks to the victors, who wrote all that history.

Alan: Thanks to Sharon for supporting and inspiring everything I do. Thanks to my kids, Parker and Emerson, for their wonderful spirits. Thanks to all three for their love and willingness to laugh at my puns. Thanks to my parents, Don and Ann Beard, for my sense of humor and the hundreds of games of Jeopardy and Trivial Pursuit that gave me just enough historical knowledge to get paid to write one-liners about it. And, of course, thanks to Alec, who is a good friend, a very funny guy, and a master at getting things done.

Alec: To my McNayr family (JoAnn, David and Joan, Joel, Hannah, and Sebastian), thank you for listening to my questionably awesome jokes for years. I can only hope seeing my name in print makes it worth it. To the Ebelings (John and Marilyn, Matt and Kim), thanks for allowing your daughter/sister to marry an artist. Thanks to decades' worth of good friends and to my Oasis family. Thank you, Alan, for guidance and friendship, and for making my sides hurt from laughter many, many times. And, finally, thank you, Katie. You're the love of my life, and my full measure of thankfulness goes to you.

image credits

v. Ryan Jones (ryanjonesart.com), Dena Flows (denaflows.com); 2. ICON: Arnab Ghoshal; 3. Ondrej Havala, Bohuslav Kotál, Christian Nunes, Linda Tanner; 4. Courtesy of NASA, BG: Nick Logan (nickaroundtheworld.wordpress.com); 5. BG: Dysartian on Flickr.com; 6. Orin Zebest, BG: mindfulseeing.com; 7. BG: rovingmagpie on Flickr.com; 8. BG: Chico Ferreira; 9. andreasreinhold.com, BG: James Watkins (flickr.com/photos/23737778@NOO); 10. Luigi from Italy, David Mitchell; 11. BG: Sarah Parga; 14. BG: Ylva Oscarsson/Poppins' Garden; 15. Photo by Mary Harrsch, BG: Philip Koopman; 16. flickr.com/photos/kyle_mancuso, BG: Amy Koller; 17. flickr.com/photos/christianstock (CC); 18. parisvega.com, BG: Peter Brooks; 23. Ben Crowe, Ireland, BG: flickr.com/photos/bensutherland; 24. © Marie-Lan Nguyen/Wikimedia Commons; 25. Photo by Mary Harrsch, BG: © 2004 Eva Ritchie; 27. Courtesy of University of Texas Libraries, The University of Texas at Austin, BG: Photo8.com; 28. BG: Eric V. Molina; 29. BG: Photo8.com; 32. Jim Champion, BG: Jim Linwood; 33. BG: Colin Berry (flickr.com/photos/cberry); 35. BG: Bernard Goldbach (insideview.ie); 37. BG: Etienne Boucher; 39. BG: Don Amaro (madeirablog.eu); 40. Courtesy of University of Texas Libraries, The University of Texas at Austin; 45. BG: Elliott Brown; 46. BG: Diane Singleton; 47. mandysmagicalworldofart.blogspot.com; 50. BG: Orin Zebest; 58. BG: Valerie Hinojosa; 62. BG: John Schanlaub; 63. BG: Ronald L. Mead; 64. Scott A. Robinson; 67. Hawking photo courtesy of NASA; 72. BG: Flavio Ferrari; 73. BG: Charles R. Loveless; 78. Wikimedia-Commons User Túrelio, RICK WESTON, flickr.com/photos/pbradyartwork; 79. BG: dustinholmes.com; 80. BG: Martin Long (muttwerks.com); 82. BG: Janusz Leszczynski; 83. BG: © 2009 Marc Osborn; 85. BG: flickr.com/photos/26392818@NOO, Bryan Hughes (twitter.com/bryanhughes); 86. BG: MANUEL FONTANEDA AMOR; 89. Hefner photo by Luke Ford; 90. juneallan.co.uk; 96. BG: Frank Escamilla (xmitter.cc); 99. BG: Michael Glasgow via flickr; 100. Milton Johanides (x-ibit-it.com), BG: Craig Vickers; 101. Robert H. Miller; 102. BG: Ken Lund; 103. Courtesy of NASA, BG: Courtesy of NASA; 106. BG: David McDaniel, Talladega, Alabama; 107: Inspired by Sean Tucker; 109. Staci Lichterman, flickr.com/photos/pontodeak; 112. Felisisima Amagna, BG: Alesia Hallmark; 113. BG: Eric Medalle; 114. Brent Snook (flickr.com/photos/fuglylogic/3486438000), BG: Sergei Donetski; 115. Gerry R. Calub; 116. Rodrigo Gonzále (flickr.com/eneas); 117. Philip Litevsky, BG: Matt Takaichi, (flickr.com/photos/touchmyichi); 118. Carl Clifford, 119. BG: Anne "Bugeaters" Reid (flickr.com/photos/bugeaters); 120. BG: Hamed Saber (saber.tel); 121. Glenn Francis (PacificProDigital.com), BG: Bryce Edwards; 127. Burns: dbking

about the authors

Self-appointed *Twitterstorians* **Alan Beard** and **Alec McNayr** are the 1–2 punch of McBeard Media, a creative and copywriting agency. Together, they've worked with clients like Nokia, Janus Capital, Alcatel-Lucent, UCLA, Pepperdine University, and the ABC Broadcast Network. They created the Historical Tweets blog in late 2008. Visit McBeardMedia.com to learn more.

AUG 1 0 2010